For Your Garden

HERB GARDENS

For Your Garden

HERB GARDENS

REBECCA W. ATWATER BRICCETTI

FRIEDMAN/FAIRFAX
PUBLISHERS

A FRIEDMAN/FAIRFAX BOOK

© 1997 by Michael Friedman Publishing Group, Inc.

Library of Congress Cataloging-in-Publication Data

Briccetti, Rebecca W. Atwater.
    Herb gardens / Rebecca W. Atwater Briccetti.
        p.   cm. -- (For your garden)
    Includes bibliographical references and index.
    ISBN 1-56799-452-0
        1. Herb gardens.   2. Herb gardening.   3. Herbs.   I. Title.
    II. Series.
    SB351.H5B6595   1997
    716--dc20   96-36147

Editor: Susan Lauzau
Art Director/Designer: Lynne Yeamans
Layout Designer: Meredith Miller
Photography Editor: Wendy Missan
Production Manager: Camille Lee

Color separations by Fine Arts Repro House Co., Ltd.
Printed in China by Leefung-Asco Printers Ltd.

10 9 8 7 6 5 4 3 2 1

For bulk purchases and special sales, please contact:
Friedman/Fairfax Publishers
Attention: Sales Department
15 West 26th Street
New York, New York 10010
212/685-6610   FAX 212/685-1307

Visit our website:
http://www.metrobooks.com

Table of Contents

INTRODUCTION

*H*erb gardens are among the oldest of recorded gardens. For thousands of years gardens were created to cultivate useful plants; the conceit of the purely ornamental garden is thought to be merely centuries old. It is their usefulness that characterizes herbs in the first place. What is an herb? It is a plant valued for some power. It may have admirable flowers or handsome foliage, but it is prized for more than that. We look to herbs for comfort and refreshment. We use them for remedies and as purifying agents. They provide dyes and inks and decoration of all kinds. Their fragrances may stimulate or soothe. And their culinary contributions are beyond reckoning.

Many plants once considered herbs are thought of as ornamentals today. Consider the rose, which has a long and venerable history in the preparation of food, remedies, and cosmetics. Petals of the apothecary's rose (Rosa gallica officinalis) have been used in astringents and antiseptics, and to treat pulmonary disease and sore throats. Other roses lend their fragrance to perfumes and potpourris. Rose water, rarely used today in Western cooking, was once indispensable. In the twentieth century, few people are accustomed to thinking of the rose as an herb, and so it is with many, many other plants. Yet the number of plants that may be considered herbs is tremendous.

Not everyone will look on the plants featured in these pages the same way. For some, their traditional characteristics as herbs will be fascinating. Others will appreciate their ornamental contributions to the flower border and tabletop arrangements. Plant them exclusively for the classic, most narrowly defined herb garden or let them provide the framework for an ornamental kitchen garden. Place them in the landscape in wildly diverse plantings. For the most part, herbs are forgiving and of fairly easy culture. Many are drought-tolerant, quite hardy, or both. If a vigorous groundcover is desired, herbs offer numerous possibilities. What group of plants is so versatile and accommodating?

ABOVE: A regal, or royal, lily (*Lilium regale*), nicotiana, and assorted herbs by the kitchen window offer fragrance to the slightest breeze. Keep culinary herbs close at hand so it isn't a chore to fetch them when in the midst of cooking.

OPPOSITE: A massive planting of purple sage at their feet makes the bright spires of desert candle (*Eremurus himalaicus*) all the more dramatic. Raised beds, in this case edged by railroad ties, have the advantage of improved drainage, and they also serve to direct attention to the plants they contain.

ABOVE: In a majestic combination, 'Hidcote' lavender and a rich red variety of pink campion (*Lychnis coronaria*) look splendid massed in the landscape.

OPPOSITE: A scattering of golden-leaved feverfew (*Tanacetum parthenium* 'Aureum') gleams in this spring tapestry. Tulips punctuate the end of a tiny path that leads to a sundial.

ABOVE: The daisylike flowers of feverfew (*Tanacetum parthenium*) are offset by herbaceous *Potentilla* and *Achillea*. Native to southeastern Europe, feverfew was brought to North America as an ornamental, and is a favorite combined with dark green foliage plants.

OPPOSITE: This evergreen bay tree (*Laurus nobilis*) in a square pot is surrounded by the soft pastels of *Pelargonium* 'Apple Blossom Orbit' and *Viola* 'Paper White'. The potted standard and radial design give this tiny garden a formal air.

ABOVE: In cottage gardens, where useful herbs and purely ornamental flowers grow chockablock, taller plants and those with more massive foliage are not always relegated to the very back row, as they are in more traditional beds.

OPPOSITE: This combination of chives (*Allium schoenoprasum*), salvia, and white-leaf everlasting, or curry plant (*Helichrysum angustifolium*), offers flowers and foliage for drying and for flavoring vinegars, salads, and other culinary offerings. It provides plenty of interesting additions to fresh flower arrangements as well.

ABOVE: A low parterre of clipped boxwood is filled with various herbs. The varying colors and textures of the herbs are reminiscent of a well-worked tapestry, proving that herbs can be used luxuriantly in even the most formal of settings.

OPPOSITE: The foliage of parsley 'Bravour' here resembles nothing so much as a miniature deciduous forest in autumn. For thousands of years, parsley has held a place of enormous importance in kitchen gardens.

Chapter One

TRADITIONAL HERB GARDENS

*T*he earliest herb gardens were enclosed and often of circular, square, or rectangular design. The classic atrium and peristyle of the ancient world eventually gave way to the courtyard and cloister, often a square with a cross at its center defined by paths. In gardens of the Middle Ages, the beds were laid out in straight lines and at right angles. Plants were grown for study, or for physical or spiritual treatment; the garden of one secluded religious order dating to the eighth century included savory, lily, poppy, iris, burdock, clary, houseleek (Sempervivum tectorum), and marsh mallow.

The Renaissance garden saw increasingly elaborate curving lines within the rectilinear framework, and symmetry—which had played an understated role in the medieval garden—became a theme of rich ornamentation. Intricate designs were created and "filled in" with contrasting plants. The axes of the Renaissance garden were usually consistent with the axes of the building around which they were designed, and the garden was intended to be viewed from a raised terrace or from within the building. Garden design of this period often featured the symmetrical pattern of planted beds known as parterres, in which the design described by living plants was grown in relief in a field of crushed stone or shells.

The knot garden, also popular about this time, featured low-growing, often shrubby plants set in interweaving geometric patterns. In mild climates, hedges of rosemary and lavender can be used to define the "knots," but boxwood, santolina, hyssop, germander, thyme, and marjoram are more commonly used.

Herb gardens of the colonial era were a far simpler affair, a reflection of the means of their owners. Though usually "working" gardens, they were often true to the love of symmetry; many were based on the popular design of a square divided into triangles by intersecting paths of brick or gravel. In the traditional herb garden today, herbs tend to dominate; or they may share the limelight with vegetables, as in the kitchen garden. Such a garden might contain a vast collection of herbs or only a few choice favorites. Yet even though the twentieth-century herb garden might be designed as nothing more complicated than a hardy border, the herb garden remains the domain of plants we single out as special.

ABOVE: Lush ribbons of chive plants fashion handsome borders for this colonial potager. The rounded flower clusters, in shades of purple, lavender, pink, or white, sit above blue-green tubular foliage that falls in soft fans. Chives offer a very effective contrast to the other members of this kitchen garden.

OPPOSITE: Geometric beds can give plants of great size or exuberant habit the room they need to thrive within the context of a rather formal garden scheme. This raised bed garden ensures well-drained soil for box, peppermint, green fennel, and spectacular bronze fennel. Raised beds are a time-honored tradition in gardening, dating at least to the middle of the fifteenth century. Gravel paths make for a well-ordered appearance and easy harvest.

ABOVE: Walkways of old brick complement garden plantings of many moods, which can be designed separately in their own compartments. In this garden, coriander, clary sage, and rosemary stand out against a formal clipped hedge.

OPPOSITE: All basil varieties thrive in sunny, well-drained locations—an excellent spot for the kitchen garden. This practical grouping, which contrasts the expected emerald green of several common basils with the dramatic purple-red of *Osimum basilicum* 'Purpurasens', makes it possible to harvest a delicious assortment for kitchen use all at once.

ABOVE: Herb garden plants needn't be confined to beds. These cheerful nasturtiums tumble around a weathered bench for a playful, rustic effect.

RIGHT: Here, a traditional circular herb garden design is punctuated at its center with an urn raised on a pedestal. Wide paths of brick give this garden scene, with its great variety of plants, a feeling of unity. The dramatic height of the urn isn't out of place, as several of the plantings themselves are quite tall, and the whole picture is backed by a stately hedge.

ABOVE: Here, an old wagon wheel provides the inspiration for a showcase of thymes, among them coconut thyme, woolly thyme, alba thyme, and clear gold thyme. It is easy to mistake a number of thyme varieties, and the spokes of this wheel keep the little "beds" quite separate, a nice idea for those who want to experiment in their cooking.

OPPOSITE: A rock wall garden can provide a growing site with excellent drainage. This ornamental planting combines the salad herbs parsley, borage, and purple basil with marigold, Johnny jump-up, and *Rosa rugosa* blossoms. Nasturtiums peek into the scene from the right. Although the plants are tucked into this rockery at various levels, all are within easy reach for harvest.

ABOVE: Perfectly straight rows give this beautifully tended vegetable garden a practical aspect, and certainly this design makes cultivation and harvesting as easy as can be. Formally clipped shrubs growing alongside the paved garden path echo the pleasing symmetry and recall the gardens of the sixteenth and seventeenth centuries, when flower and vegetable beds grew side by side in stylized parterres.

ABOVE: Culinary herbs, here a trio of thymes—golden, purple variegated, and white—are best grown in quantity if they are to be harvested regularly. A billowing profusion of growth spills over the sides of these geometrical raised beds.

ABOVE: In this enchanting English garden, such medieval herb-garden plants as fennel and foxglove (*Digitalis lutea*) grow in a more contemporary border setting. This bed's relaxed feel lends itself well to the more natural landscaping of many gardens today.

OPPOSITE: This arrangement of jewel-toned herbs rivals that of any flower border, with all the variety of texture a gardener could wish for. The happy confusion of fennel, purple sage, various alliums, and lavender (*Lavandula stoechas*) is kept quietly in check with traditional pavers set in orderly fashion.

ABOVE: This potager combines the decorative effect of a formal parterre with the virtues of a working kitchen garden. A standard gooseberry punctuates the little central disk. Individual beds supply the owners with such diverse crops as onions, sorrel, and mint, and fragrant honeysuckle abundantly covers the fence.

OPPOSITE: A popular theme is that of the Shakespeare garden, which features plants mentioned by the author in his plays and poems. Planted in these lush beds formally crisscrossed by stone paths are sweet cicely, alecost (*Chrysanthemum balsamita* or *Balsamita major*), and the ever-popular fennel. The style of this garden, with its rectilinear layout and low-growing, clipped borders, complements that of the house even though it is not a slavish period reproduction.

Chapter Two

HERBS IN THE LANDSCAPE

*I*n recent centuries it has been the fashion to confine herbs to gardens devoted exclusively to their kind—that is, gardens of "useful" plants. But remembering that the plants we know as herbs hail from scores of families and are amazingly diverse, it should come as no surprise that many of them stand beautifully on their own and look marvelous when integrated into the rest of the garden. After all, you can choose among herbs anything from shrubs and even trees to groundcovers. They offer flowers of every description, and often foliage that is beautifully ornamental, perhaps with unusual texture or intriguing shape, glaucous or in beguiling tones of blue.

In mixed borders, larger groupings of herbs make an impressive display. In perennial gardens, many herbs can be called on to provide contrast and to fill in where immature plantings have yet to grow. Many of the shorter plants are pretty in an uncommon way for edging walkways or beds; the tallest can make striking accents in the landscape. And for the fancier of the wildflower, hummingbird, or butterfly garden, herbs are simply indispensable.

ABOVE: Herbs and ornamentals spill over the sides of this time-worn brick walkway. The low, mounding habit of many herbs makes them convenient companions around a garden seat, from which the butterflies and bees they attract can be enjoyed.

OPPOSITE: A sundial, reached by stepping stones that are nearly overgrown, stands in this romantic herbaceous border, which includes feverfew, santolina, violets, and French lavender. It is easy to forget the working nature of herbs when we see them so gracefully integrated into such a magnificent composition.

ABOVE: Thyme, planted among the paving stones in this quiet corner, acts in concert with a sundial to make the age-old pun on "time." A rustic bench offers a serene spot for contemplation.

ABOVE: Mounds of cranesbill (*Geranium psilostemon*) and golden marjoram (*Origanum vulgare* 'Aureum') are anchors in this fabulous garden planned around yellows, greens, and white. The herb isn't tucked into an inconspicuous corner, but is literally allowed to shine.

ABOVE: The accommodating climate of the Pacific Northwest coaxes a wide variety of ornamentals and herbs to perform at their best. Stately yellow iris are answered at the back of this garden by foxgloves, and fennel and roses are unexpected companions in the foreground.

OPPOSITE: Herbs integrated into this extraordinary border are on a par with the best-known of ornamentals. Featured here are *Euphorbia characias, E. wulfenii,* purple sage, *Kniphofia* 'August Yellow', and *Artemisia* 'White Windows'. The sage makes a striking contribution.

ABOVE: These white tulips are spotlit by lemon balm. Where climate allows, tuck herbs into the spring flower border. They'll offer a longer season of usefulness with such an early start, and the variety of foliage will be most welcome.

LEFT: A ramble through an earthly paradise reveals a splashy planting of herbs. *Nepeta sibirica* weaves among plantings of two roses—*Rosa gallica officinalis* and *R. mundi*—resulting in a scene so saturated with color that it looks as though it were drawn in pastels.

ABOVE: Many herbs make excellent underplantings. Here, individual orange trees are centered in their own little beds.

OPPOSITE: A slope covered with relatively easygoing plants is a practical answer to erosion. When considering an alternative to grass, let your imagination run wild. Few herbs demand meticulous attention, and many are quite water-thrifty.

ABOVE: In this nod to the cottage garden, flowers in every shade of purple are offset by a great diversity of foliage, much of it a bright lime green. It is the dramatic heads of flowering chives (*Allium*) that get the most attention here.

RIGHT: Border "hedges" of 'Hidcote' lavender line the axes of a formal composition that features standard roses. Sorrel (*Rumex*), a tender green with a bright, acidic flavor, surrounds a potted olive tree. In a mild climate, a garden such as this can be enjoyed for many months.

ABOVE: This little planting of herbs and ornamentals is a living nosegay. The hot colors of red and orange-gold are more than matched by the enthusiastic diversity of foliage. Flower umbels of dill add an airy note to an otherwise dense collection.

OPPOSITE: Columbine (*Aquilegia*), alecost (*Chrysanthemum balsamita*), catmint (*Nepeta*), and wormwood (*Artemisia absinthum*) are combined in this beautifully designed Shakespeare garden, a collection with great variety of foliage and flower.

ABOVE: Rosemary (*Rosmarinus officinalis*) and thick-leaf phlox (*Phlox carolina* 'Chattahoochee') seem unusual partners at this entryway, perhaps because rosemary's culinary fame overshadows its distinguished past as an ornamental. It will grow quite shrubby, and lends itself nicely to topiary.

LEFT: A hedge gateway invites the visitor into this stunning garden of purples and pinks. *Nepeta* and *Dianthus* traditionally appear in perennial borders such as these. Depending on the species (of which there are hundreds), *Dianthus* can offer rich, spicy fragrance, blue-green foliage, and abundant flowering, all in one rather low-growing plant that masses beautifully. *D. caryophyllus*, known as clove pink for its fragrance, was used to scent and flavor cosmetic and medicinal preparations for centuries.

Chapter Three

THE WORKING NATURE OF HERBS

*P*lant a variety of herbs, and you will not exhaust the possibilities for their uses for a long while. A home supply of herbs is a delirious resource for anyone with an interest in cooking or handicrafts. There is nothing more inspiring to the cook than a garden full of flavorful herbs, which are delightful in salads, sauces, soups, and indeed almost any dish. In the depths of winter, dried herbs rekindle the fresh tastes of summer, easing us through harsh and unruly weather with promises that the garden will prosper again.

As adornments for wreaths, bouquets, and other ornamental arrangements, herbs—both fresh and dried—have their decorative uses outside the garden. They also make a fragrant and colorful contribution to many potpourris and perfumes.

Traditionally, herbs have also been used in soothing teas as well as medicinally in syrups and extractions. The dual nature of these time-honored plants, which are both ornamental and hardworking, makes them extraordinarily rewarding garden dwellers.

ABOVE: Anise hyssop (*Agastache foeniculum*), planted in generous clumps, makes itself noticed in the garden; when the plant—also known as blue or fennel giant hyssop—is happy, it may reach three feet (90cm) tall. A hardy member of the mint family and not a true hyssop, it is unrelated to the plant that flavored homemade cough syrups. The clean green leaves, which may be dried for use in cooking and in making tea, have a complex flavor that, like licorice or anise, seems faintly sweet. The flowers make pretty garnishes and are delicious in baked goods and sautés; they grow in substantial purple spikes that attract butterflies, bees, and hummingbirds in mid- to late summer.

OPPOSITE: Chamomile and other herbs provide a ground-covering carpet beneath the branches of this standard gooseberry. A standard of any kind is an elegant accent for a circular bed, and any number of low-growing herbs would serve double duty planted around the base, in the place of the more usual flowering annuals.

ABOVE: As a cooking herb, parsley (*Petroselinum crispum*) is immensely valuable when fresh; for use when dried, it is best to select the more flavorful broad-leafed variety. Parsley looks equally attractive in formal and informal designs; it has been used to edge gardens for thousands of years. Plant it in great, soft mounds or tidy rows, but plant it in quantity. It appreciates a nitrogen-rich soil and good sun.

ABOVE: In early to midsummer, chamomile produces tiny, daisy-like flowers, long used in soothing teas and other preparations. The soft, almost wispy foliage forms a feathery mound when plants are set close together. Roman chamomile (*Chamaemelum nobile*) and German, or sweet false, chamomile (*Matricaria recutita*) look much alike. German chamomile, a true annual, can reach two feet (60cm) in height, producing flowers less bitter than those of the one-foot (30cm) Roman chamomile, a tender perennial. Roman chamomile foliage is often described as apple-scented.

ABOVE: Lemon mint (*Mentha xpiperita*, also known as *M. citrata*) goes by the common name of bergamot mint as well. The leaves of this somewhat shorter (eighteen to twenty-four inches [45 to 60cm]) peppermint variety have a lemony aroma when bruised. The commercial zenith of lemon mint was eighteenth-century France, where it was used in the preparation of a vast array of cosmetics, perfumes, and potpourris. In the garden, it offers masses of lush emerald growth that can be held in check—if, for example, bordered by bricks or paving stones.

ABOVE: Harvest lavender where it grows in profusion, to avoid stripping the plants. Slender flower spikes and narrow leaves make lavender an elegant addition to cut-flower arrangements; the combination of dusty, faded purple blossoms and gray-green leaves is sophisticated, whether fresh or dried. Lavender is the herb of choice for scenting linens and soaps, and culinary tradition in some parts of the world, perhaps most famously Provence, uses it to flavor savories and sweets.

ABOVE LEFT: Chicory flowers, composed of delicate purple, daisylike rays, emerge along weedy, open stems. Their spare contribution is prettiest in combination with more fulsome plants. Members of the chicory family have been enjoyed in cooking for thousands of years—the leaves in salads, the roots eaten boiled or raw as a vegetable, or roasted and ground as a coffee substitute (of debatable success). *Cichorium* has historically been used as a medicine in treating heart and circulatory ailments.

ABOVE RIGHT: Scented geraniums (*Pelargonium*) number more than two hundred, and a tremendous variety of fragrances are commercially available. Choose from geraniums with scents reminiscent of citrus and spices of many kinds, various nuts, mints, stone fruits, ginger, and rose, among others. New hybrids appear with every passing year. The foliage can look as glorious as it smells, sometimes elaborately ruffled, variegated, or handsomely margined. Scented geraniums thrive in the garden (provide for good air circulation), and brought indoors in containers, their rich fragrance can be enjoyed close at hand.

LEFT: This corner of a kitchen garden features a pretty arrangement of chives, feverfew, and santolina. Various cultures, among them Chinese, Arab, and western European, have found medicinal uses for these herbs over the years. Today santolina, or lavender cotton, is more valued as an ornamental that lends itself to neat management; it has long been used in knot gardens. The very bitter nature of feverfew discourages any use but therapeutic, leaving chives the sole member of this grouping truly welcome at the table.

ABOVE: What garden would be complete without dill (*Anethum graveolens*)? It has a distinguished presence in the herb garden, and is a soft and starry addition to the back of the flower border. The yellow-green flower umbels are fireworks displays in miniature. The foliage and flowers taste of the very essence of summer, and the richly fragrant seeds keep handily to flavor breads, salads, soups, and pickles in the cooler months. A rewarding herb to raise from seed, dill should be sown where it is intended to grow, as it doesn't like to be transplanted.

ABOVE: The flowers of garlic chives (*Allium tuberosum*) resemble those of certain heat-loving, subtropical bulbs, but these plants are much more accepting of variable weather. Harvest young leaves (wider and flatter than those of the herb simply known as "chives") for the gentle flavor of garlic they add to foods. The blooms make a stunning addition to flower arrangements.

RIGHT: No herb is so winning when eaten fresh, nor so disappointing by contrast when dried, as basil. Sweet basil 'Green Ruffles' (*Ocimum basilicum*) is one of the huge number of cultivars commercially available. The flavors of lemon, cinnamon, and anise basils make a nice change, and basils with purple foliage are a delight. Thai basil produces delicious leaves as long as three inches (7cm), and at eighteen to twenty-four inches (45 to 60cm) tall, is a handsome foliage plant in the landscape; it is described as tasting of mint and cloves. As basil is rather slow to grow from seed, you may want to seek out young plants for your garden.

LEFT: The purple-blue flowers of borage *(Borago officinalis),* which droop from delicately hairy stems, are a beautiful garnish for salads and cooling summer drinks, and crystallized or fresh, they're a nice alternative to expensive candied violets. Dried in silica, they make pretty (though inedible) decorations for wreaths and other handicrafts. Borage is thought by some to be a good companion plant with a degree of natural pest repellent, so consider planting it among more susceptible plants.

RIGHT: The root of purple coneflower *(Echinacea purpurea)* has long been used in the treatment of fever and infection, and current research is investigating how it strengthens the immune system. A favorite plant for the perennial flower border, *Echinacea* usually flowers about three feet (90cm) off the ground with pink-to-purple rays surrounding a dramatic central cone. Of interest to those who enjoy their gardens primarily at twilight, a white form is available. The plant is native to North American prairies.

RIGHT: Garden sage (*Salvia officinalis*), historically thought to prolong life, is vital to the herb garden of any cook. The elongated, faintly downy, silvered foliage is very aromatic and essential in many poultry, meat, bread, and soup recipes. A tender perennial shrub, the plant typically grows two to two and a half feet (60–75cm) tall. Sage is handsome in combination with many other border and kitchen garden plants, and happily there is a wide selection from which to choose, among them purple sage, scarlet sage, variegated sage (with white and green; gold and green; or green, purple-pink, and white leaves), Mexican sage (*S. leucantha*), pineapple sage (*S. elegans*), and clary sage (*S. sclarea*). Give sage a sunny location with fast-draining soil.

LEFT: One way to control the exuberant nature of mint is to plant it in a container, to prevent it from spreading and crowding out its neighbors. Here, glossy leaves are in bright contrast to an old bucket. You have only to bruise mint foliage slightly to release the powerful aroma. A collection of easygoing mints might include lemon, apple, pineapple, and chocolate mint, in addition to the classic peppermint and spearmint.

ABOVE: This bright jumble was designed as an edible garden. Nasturtiums weave through a company of lettuce, salvia, and *Calendula* 'Orange King' and 'Neon'. Plant combinations are happiest when all the individuals share cultural preferences. These sun-lovers offer an arresting variety of foliage types.

OPPOSITE: A golden-leafed cultivar of marjoram (*Origanum vulgare* 'Aureum', also known as golden oregano) in a graceful terra-cotta pot highlights the meticulous caretaking of this potager. The potting mixture can be formulated to whatever the inhabitant of the pot likes best—in this case, a free-draining, somewhat sandy blend.

ABOVE LEFT: The yellow-green leaves of lemon balm (*Melissa officinalis*) hint at their uncannily lemony fragrance. Bees are keenly interested in the small, white flowers, hence another common name for the plant, bee balm. The toothed leaves are the basis for a famously soothing French infusion, and have been used in numerous medicinal preparations. Fresh lemon balm is delicious in dressings and stuffings, drinks cold and hot, soups, and fruit dishes.

ABOVE RIGHT: *Thymus doerfleri* fashions a creeping carpet of enthusiastic purplish blossoms. This wildly flowering ornamental is generally easygoing, and is happy when sited in a sunny, well-drained spot.

LEFT: This serene study in soft purples is composed of blue *Viola* and hardy catmint (*Nepeta faassenii*).

OPPOSITE: The fiery color of the hips and haws of numerous plants captures the attention of hungry wildlife. These make beautiful additions to such handicrafts as wreaths. The brilliant hips of *Rosa rugosa*, rich in Vitamin C, are sought for the making of an excellent jelly, and are delicious in teas and baked goods.

Chapter Four

AN HERB FOR EVERY GARDEN

Whatever the situation in which you garden, herbs can play supporting or starring roles, as you choose. They offer myriad possibilities for naturalistic and formal gardens alike, and herbs can likewise work their magic in gardens of all sizes. The smallest corner is large enough for a garden. Window boxes and woodland paths, modest cottage gateways and imposing gravel courtyards, around birdbaths and by the seashore, all these are wonderful places to enjoy herbs. For the contrast they offer in texture, for their magnificent variety of foliage, flower, and fragrance, herbs belong in every garden.

ABOVE: Lady's mantle (*Alchemilla mollis*), purple sage, chives in full flower, and poppies create an exuberant little border that sits between a path of old brick and a wooden fence of soft green. Small though this growing area is, it will make a nice contribution to floral arrangements and in the kitchen.

OPPOSITE: A walled terrace offers a sheltered climate with the benefit of warmer temperatures. Steps positioned near the wall make it possible to arrange plants at various heights and change the garden picture on a whim, rather than relying entirely on the hope that the plants will grow into the desired effect.

LEFT: The gold-tinged lichen growing on this venerable stone bench is echoed in the variegated foliage of the shrub and in the diminutive herb garden at its feet. With its symmetry and tiny standard at its center, this minute garden is quite at home in its stately surroundings.

BELOW: This weathered stone trough is kept company by a host of terra-cotta pots of various sizes. Foxgloves call attention to the picturesque stone wall that marks the garden boundary.

OPPOSITE: A single strawberry pot is home to variegated nasturtiums, catmint, Johnny jump-ups, variegated thyme, and scented-leaf geraniums. An imaginative variety of plantings isn't limited by lack of space.

ABOVE: Thriving in the radiant heat from a stone wall, creeping Jenny, houseleek, scented-leaf geranium, mint, thyme, and purple sage are clustered to create a container garden. The individual plants provide different shades of green, ranging from tones of yellow-white through blue-green, to purple.

ABOVE: A romantic notion, this garden seat is planted with fragrant chamomile. The little plants are resilient enough to survive frequent visitation. Chamomile can be grown over footpaths, too, releasing wonderful scent with every step.

RIGHT: What thyme may lack in height, it more than makes up for in impact. With such luxuriant flowering as this, it can be relied on to glorify any sunny corner.

ABOVE: Less contained than it is punctuated by an iron fence, this planting gives the impression of a cottage garden. A path of lavender in shades of deep amethyst contrasts handsomely with the yellow stone of the house. The herb can be harvested judiciously from a border hedge of this generous size without spoiling the effect.

ABOVE: A garden such as this, with a strong sense of design and structure provided by paved paths and hedges, can be as enticing in winter as it is in summer; even in a harsher climate, without the pretty sight of the plants so fancifully frosted, the "bones" of this garden would ensure an interesting picture. Thoughtful pruning gives the trees their exquisite silhouettes, a natural foil to the formal style of this spacious, quiet refuge.

OPPOSITE: This seaside garden uses a natural rock formation as a "planter," an opportunity to improve the soil to the inhabitants' liking. Because wind off the ocean carries with it a good deal of salt, the most delicate of herbs should be reserved for more protected locations.

RIGHT: Window boxes, casual almost by definition, are ideal for patchwork plantings that bring together fruits, herbs, and ornamentals. This summer combination includes upright, mounding, and trailing plants.

BELOW: Include herbs in a wildlife garden. Many—such as alliums, roses, coneflowers, salvias, lavender, and nasturtiums—attract butterflies, hummingbirds, and bees. A diverse plant community makes an attractive habitat for many small creatures in search of food and shelter.

ABOVE: Where space is not at a premium, gardeners are free to include anything they desire. A paving of large, smooth pebbles makes harvesting from this garden a simple task even when rain has turned the soil to mud. Planning has made for easy access to each of these plant groupings.

ABOVE: A garden lavishly planted in front of the house is at once beautiful and practical. The herbs growing here are but a step from the doorway. With areas for strolling and for restful contemplation, this closely planted garden is also fairly drought-tolerant, without a water-guzzling lawn of high-maintenance grass.

INDEX

PHOTO CREDITS

©Derek Fell: 17, 19, 31

©John Glover: 10, 13, 15, 18, 20 left, 20-21, 32, 38, 39, 40 left, 48 both, 51 top and bottom left, 55 left, 64, 65 both, 66, 67, 69 both

©Dency Kane: 22, 23, 42, 47, 51 top right, 53 both, 54 both

©Charles Mann: 12, 24, 34, 49, 50, 52

©Clive Nichols: 2 (The Old Rectory, Northamptonshire), 6 (Turn End Garden, Haddenham, Buckinghamshire), 7 (designed by Sue Berger, Bristol), 8 (Longacre, Kent), 9, 11 (designed by Nigel Colborn), 14 (The Daily Telegraph Garden, Chelsea, 1991), 16 (Le Manoir Aux Quat Saisons, Oxfordshire), 25 (Le Manoir Aux Quat Saisons, Oxfordshire), 26 (designed by Nuala Hancock and Mathew Bell, Chelsea, 1994), 27 (Hadspen House Garden and Nursery, Somerset), 28 (Bourton House, Gloucestershire), 29 (designed by Mark Brown), 30 (designed by Joan Murdy), 35 (White Windows, Hampshire), 36-37 (The Old Rectory, Northamptonshire), 37 right, 40-41 (Le Manoir Aux Quat Saisons, Oxfordshire), 43 (designed by Mark Brown), 44-45 (The Anchorage, Kent), 46 (Bourton House, Gloucestershire), 55 right, 56 (HMP Leyhill Garden, Hampton Court, 1995), 57 (designed by Julie Toll, Chelsea, 1994), 58 top left, top right (Hexham Herbs, Northumberland) and bottom (Sticky Wicket, Dorset), 59, 60 (Monk Sherbourne Horticultural Society, Chelsea, 1993), 61 (designed by Daniel Pearson Evening Standard Garden, Chelsea, 1994), 62 top (Barnsley House, Gloucestershire), 62 bottom (Redenham Park, Hampshire), 63

©Jerry Pavia: 33, 45 right

©Nance Trueworthy: 68, 70, 71